4/18

Little
Pebble™

Little Critters

Spiders

CAPSTONE PRESS
a capstone imprint

Little Pebble is published by Capstone Press,
1710 Roe Crest Drive, North Mankato, Minnesota 56003
www.mycapstone.com

Library of Congress Cataloging-in-Publication Data
Names: Amstutz, Lisa J., author.
Title: Spiders / by Lisa Amstutz.
Other titles: Little pebble. Little critters.
Description: North Mankato, Minnesota : Capstone Press, a Capstone imprint,
    [2018] | Series: Little pebble. Little critters | Audience: Ages 4–8. |
    Audience: K to grade 3. | Includes bibliographical references and index.
Identifiers: LCCN 2016051633| ISBN 9781515778264 (library binding) | ISBN
    9781515778394 (pbk.) | ISBN 9781515778431 (eBook PDF)
Subjects: LCSH: Spiders—Juvenile literature.
Classification: LCC QL458.4 .A47 2018 | DDC 595.4/4—dc23
LC record available at https://lccn.loc.gov/2016051633

Editorial Credits
Gena Chester, editor; Sarah Bennett, designer;
Wanda Winch, media researcher; Tori Abraham, production specialist

Photo Credits
Dreamstime: G3miller, 17; Shutterstock: Aleksey Stemmer, spider web background, 3, 24,
Calin Tatu, 9, Cathy Keifer, 11, 15, 19, Comel Constantin, 1, Dirk Ercken, 13, Jen Helton,
cover, Panu Ruangjan, 5, Radka Palenikova, 22, RealNoi, 7, Worraket, 21

Printed in China.
010419F17

Table of Contents

Many Legs

Look!

It's a spider!

It has eight legs.

Its body has two parts.

Some spiders are big.

Some are tiny.

Most have eight eyes.

Spiders make silk.

It is strong. It is sticky.

Silk makes spider webs.

Time to Eat

Webs trap bugs.

Spiders eat the bugs.

Yum!

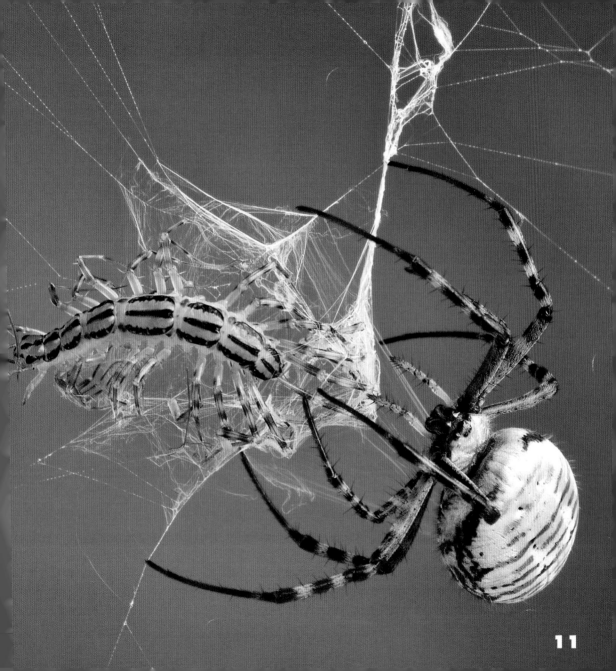

Some spiders hunt for food.

They hide and jump.

They eat frogs.

They eat mice too.

Munch!

Spiders bite their prey.

They have fangs.

fangs

Some spiders can bite
people. Ouch!
But most will not hurt you.

17

Growing Up

Spiders lay eggs.

A silk sac holds the eggs.

It keeps them safe.

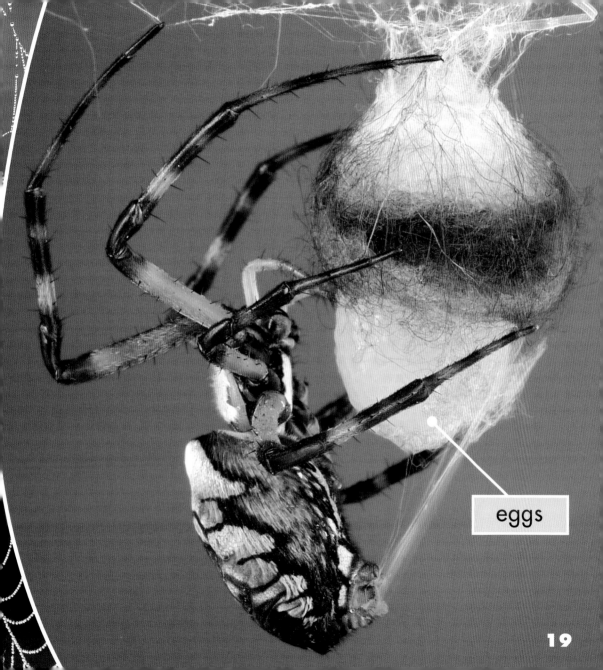

eggs

19

Baby spiders hatch out.

Can you count them?

Off they go!

Glossary

fang—a long, pointed tooth

hatch—to come out of an egg

prey—an animal hunted by another animal for food

sac—a bag made of silk that holds a spider's eggs

silk—thread that is made by a spider

Read More

Borgert-Spaniol, Megan. *Spiders.* Backyard Wildlife. Minneapolis, Bellwether Media, 2014.

Herrington, Lisa M. *It's a Good Thing There Are Spiders.* New York: Scholastic Inc., 2015.

Smith, Sian. *Spiders.* Creepy Critters. North Mankato, Minn.: Capstone Publishing, 2014.

Internet Sites

FactHound offers a safe, fun way to find Internet sites related to this book. All of the sites on FactHound have been researched by our staff.

Here's all you do:
Visit *www.facthound.com*
Type in this code: 9781515778264

Check out projects, games and lots more at
www.capstonekids.com

Critical Thinking Questions

1. Why do spiders make webs?
2. What do spiders eat?
3. What is a fang?

Index

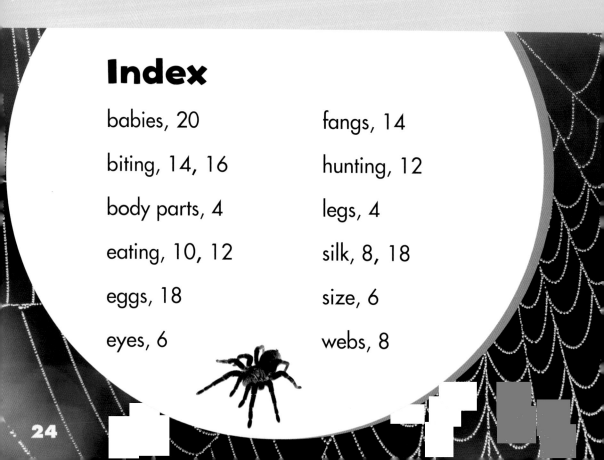